Deep Colour

Deep Colour

Diana Bridge

OTAGO UNIVERSITY PRESS
Te Whare Tā o Te Wānanga o Ōtākou

for Vincent

... if the thought really yielded to the object, if its attention were on the object, not on its category, the very objects would start talking under the lingering eye.

— THEODOR ADORNO

... from his pictures I have learned how it is essential to gaze far beneath the surface, that art is nothing without patient handiwork, and that there are many difficulties to be reckoned with in the recollection of things.

— W.G. SEBALD

Contents

I

Deep colour

Somewhere down there in the aquarium, gleaming
like a bit of neon, the tiny floating scarf of a fin.
Deep colour, the words for it are out of range –
that much I can tell you. What I cannot say
is how a life gathers its themes.

The twist of colour twirls, it comes to me
like a lost strand in the plait of ancestry. Should I try
and pin it down or avoid it on account of what might
lie there? They would tell me not to know is loss.
Would they send me back to yesterday?

I have no attachment to that opaque throng,
only one or two of whom stand out from the murk
of the tank. The atrocities of the past lie there,
compacted to a single bed. Day after day
the past waits for the present to fall

into its hands. One truth will soon displace
another; I am left with this. A life gathers its themes,
some of which it may never weave. Deep colour
twirls in the tank, standing in for what I didn't ask.
Now she is gone and not to know is loss.

Two poems *in memoriam* Jane Hunter

A split sky

I stand to one side watching as shadow
fills the shallow basin of the lawn
taking the great trees with it

trees that were her backdrop
I would be content with outline   sharp
in the light   to speak of her now

requires precision   I call on splinters
of conversation   snippets
of scene   re-open them to view

then piece them back into some new
assemblage   which works only to expose
fresh vacancies   images of separation

possess our landscape   a disc
bisects the evening blue
its pale curve heavy   the split sky

solid   the scene above our heads
material in a way she cannot be
again   the joining and

the severing endlessly renew

Moving through leaves

what breathes in the trees
when she is gone –
not Daphne

yet   I have seen her moving
through leaves
the dark of magnolia

a switched child   returned
to her Indian years
her cloud of hair burns

a temple light   against bleached
stone   as she flutters down
a flight of steps

body paused   a phrase quicksilver
on the wind's current   reminding
me   she is open to words

though she is well beyond my reach
and   I believed   allusion
in that instant   I match her to one

what breathes in the trees
when she is gone   like Daphne
not to be won

Freestanding

My friend, true poet, breathes in metaphor and gives it back
quickened by interruption. When next we share
the rich precarious balance of our lives
I'll tell her I was Turner, reading the currents of the air,
getting the first strokes down, when I felt the baby
steady herself against my legs; that I was stopped then
by her upturned face, dazzled, overcome, by two
top teeth that broke in tiny crescents from a gum.

Right now, there is a tugging at my knee.
What story was it started with a smile like hers?
This baby girl is named for gold; a cap
of thickening hair confirms it. Without warning
one hand leaves my knee, and then she is freestanding –
the topmost tier of the cabbage tree, six frantic hands
mad with applause to back her. A line of virgin images bursts
from my brain. Come, Xanthe, fan the flames.

She spends time with objects

1

From the lawn where she is playing she spots a glittering chip.
She lifts it from its gravel bed and sets it on a step
beside a cherry stone, next to a shard of shell. Smiling,
she pounces on a piece of broken plastic and adds it to her heap.
She is immersed in making her own class of object.
Each item is selected for its small, sharp, solid body.
She tests her choices with her teeth.

A synthesis of senses prods her into action.
Attentive, free of bias, she lessens the space
between items. I do the opposite.
I look into the distance as I attach to objects
meanings steeped in feeling. My choices
harbour differences and antique schisms.
Like me, they war within.

2

When the earthquake came, it struck like revolution.
It threw the statue on its face, chipping the cool grey plaster,
gashing an eyelid and laying bare a portion of the nose.
A line that might have been inflicted by a bullwhip
now cuts through lip and chin. Below the bud
of shoulders the semi-circle of the base
has crumbled to a coastline abraded by its waves.

I stand the lovely frail statue on a square of yellow,
its high pile faced with green, thinking that flowers might
be placed there, as everywhere in Asia offerings
are set in front of statues. But who would sweep a pile
of dying roses into a selvedge, who place before
the Buddha sallow orchids, their skirts drawn
back from curling silken tongues? I am the one

who would invest each thing with meaning –
how would the Buddha care? I wipe the label 'damaged'
from my statue and watch the marks that score it
change into a spatter of white petals. As yin
and yang entwine on the ancient symbol, the way
that opposites have always done, the pale clay merges
with its plaster, surface and core now one.

Her sort of order

She sits looking out on a remote
unblemished blue   the green of the garden
the breakneck slide of the hillside

down to the bay   in the ten minutes left
before supper   she will draw her eyes
back to the lightly ordered clutter

of the room   reclining on her desk
in gradations of the colours of the rainbow
lies a sheaf of narrow pens

laid out   like a margin for a manuscript
its words familiar   not yet   language
scattered   through her text

        are headstones   across
their oblong faces crawl swirls of cursive type
        a cloud of chaos threatens

as she waits for it to   still   she remembers
        a directive designed to
light what loiters   lost   in calligraphic corridors

processing is my primary occupation   followed up
by *making metaphor my next*   it is a signal for
her thoughts to rise   as singular as

coloured pens   they call to her like sirens
in all the shades and half-shades of the rainbow
tips dusted with glitter

He has put away pointers

Camille Pissarro's Le Champ de choux, Pontoise, *1873*

1

He says it is morning – but is it? I love best
what I cannot pin down: a direction, a thickness –
greenish-blue ribbons coasting to somewhere outside
my vision but, somehow, contained in the frame.
It comes down to a rectangle holding in balance
its luminous layers, to a field made fast by a foreground
of cabbages, and the way that the cabbages tumble
like hedgehogs under a downpour of light.

2

The trees at the edge of the scene are as dark as Hades.
Deepest black on slightly less black. The leafless trunk nearest,
a stick insect with two dozen legs, recedes
where the head would be. Phasmid to phantom.
Come down from the clouds! He won't have a bar of it.
He doesn't look sideways or back. If he journeys at all,
it's to regions of colour contained in the one word black.
It's to balance the whitening sky that he brings in blackness,

to offset three lit trees. One, a cone that is picked out in light,
is re-shawled in a cyan haze. It rises like smoke from jade.
You needn't look up – it's no form in a niche.
You don't have to ask yourself what kind of tree
would wear a mandorla. He has put away pointers.
When a woman serene as Ceres in summer stands in a gloaming,
she's a pillar that earths the light. Two stooped forms
on the edge of the manifest are stabs at the moment.

They join with the visible blue of the air, the bright side
of a woman's head. The light is a leveller binding the scene,
radiant hoops of cabbage to the quivering line
of the sky, ourselves to the gorgeously muted surface.
He insists on no more than that. Even so,
there are times when I bring to a primrose flush
cupped in the fork of a tree the warmth of a daughter's face
drawn into, or up from, the darkness.

Singapore shapes

Her pram is a walled garden open to everything that waves
in spikes and fronds over her head. She is assembling
her own legacy of shapes. Caped shoulders, trumpet mouths,
marbles of monsoon rain. Driven as Eve,
she reaches for the gloss on leaves, the distant leap

of monkeys. Is there a category called 'movement'
in her mind, a place for still and never still?
Bedrock or residue, what pictures will she keep
when she comes home? What comfort
will they give when she is cold, displaced, allergic?

A caterpillar plans its drop into her pram.
I sit on a sandstone wall below a tree, my shoulder
spotted with the traces of its tiny temporary legs.
Frangipani flowers fall about her feet. The birds
are the reds-and-yellows of new memories.

The professional

for Will, Ben and George

She has observed the rhythm of their long brown legs
as they walk into the open, treading a bridge
that unrolls out of the trees. She grasps the way

their bodies quarter-turn towards each other, holding close
a joke they think no one could ever understand.
The bush brackets their absorption, their quality of being

brothers – not just any brothers, but the two younger
of a trio. A whole head taller, the eldest walks
immersed in secret thought a half a step behind.

Like the photographer, he sees formation
as a calculated action and to preserve
the threesome walks to his brothers' right.

Singing robes

Early spring is here. A simple concept or assumption
has become as faceted as water below the layered overhang
of leaves. Spring has made me open-minded.

A thick, disfiguring vein of cable that swoops through
branches has become determined as a vine.
There is a sureness to the way the neighbour's roofline

is extended by the still bared limbs of our late-flowering trees.
Among massed colour – magnolia, rhododendron
and camellia – one bright bush stands out.

Its colour is explicit, candid even, but a word has been
withheld, a single word. I don't want to track it,
any more than see abundance yield itself to pattern.

A feather ripples on a surface deepened by light.
Must you tie it all to something? If I were Wordsworth,
I would think you must, for fear that spring be wasted.

A butterfly floats in the paint

A British Blue's nature is puzzling; we're not sure
how he figures things out. He has fathomed our talk's
direction, and leapt lightly on to a ledge. It's a high
narrow shelf meant for objects. Suspended above,
a shield affixed to the wall, is a gleaming sun-shaped
circle, but darker and cooler than sun. Crossing
the circle's surface, as though passing through life,
is a symbol unknown to Achilles – a butterfly
floats in the paint, empty of all but its soul.

Gus knows about transformation; paws tucked, tail
wrapped, his soft oblong shape has converted into a plinth.
Yellow eyes on the butterfly's outline, he dreams of being
winged. A cat's passion lies in pursuit, we think.
When his beautiful blue-grey body is struck by a car
and left on the side of a street, we see him as more
like the Chinese sage who loved roaming for roaming's
sake; and know that he, like Zhuangzi, who woke,
unmoored, from dream, has merged with that butterfly,
subject or object, but emptied of all but its soul.

Here comes my soul

Would rebirth be enough for you?
Oh, baby, anything at all would do.

Move over now, here comes my soul,
flap, slap, doing a Charleston of happiness.

The flying creatures

for Dame Judi Dench, Eleanor Slade, and Bob

It was the glimmering white screen that drew them
into the clearing. The ecologist picked one off.
At first I didn't catch its name. But I knew hers.
I knew a voice tempered to trap or cosset.
She might never before have held a beetle black
as tropical night, but she stroked its crescent
horns and praised it for its planetary role.
Then she dropped her voice

and relayed quiet comfort to a creature
ambushed by its destination, a beetle,
species 'dung', name 'Bob', that had flung itself
in the way of white transcendence.

II
Utamaro's Objects

In the New York Public Library

I was inside the tabernacle, waiting.
I had pulled on white gloves and propped
my elbows like a mantis on the shining desk –
teak, I thought, but I am no examiner of woods.
They brought in *Gifts from the Ebb Tide*,
a delicate taxonomy of the sea's leavings.

In the shifts of wind-blown autumn, shells
became symbols of impermanence. Shell-seekers
swooped on the brittle treasures before they were sucked
back and under. One page showed the fleeting
season and its rituals of gathering, the transience
and the harvesting to be savoured side by side.

Songs of the garden

1
true forms

From a child he loved to watch a cricket's wings vibrate
against its haunches. He saw how wings unfurl to fly
and fold in sleep. When it lay level on a leaf,
he noticed the high-angled legs that bracketed
each creature's thorax; the way an oval body
straightened to hop, extended to lay and lengthened
as it aged. They said that he had learned
the true forms even from larvae.

When he came to read the Chinese manuals, he discovered
that 'where there are flowers there should be
butterflies, as a fine lady is accompanied by her maids'.
And so he passed from flowers to insects.

2
residents of the garden

Each resident of Utamaro's garden flaunts the freshness
of the moment. As it peeks through screens of foliage
or hovers over lifting, coiling, waving leaves, every cricket,
katydid or beetle glimpsed from the side, a rat snake
circling its page, even the reflected frog that hangs, all
but eclipsed, below a lily-pad reveals a mid-life poise
and balance. Here are creatures caught on the wing
before they can transform, mutate or age.

Poems play as they like with nature's shifts and turns.
His prints hold only the green of summer. I would settle
for a present as crisp and charismatic as Utamaro's.
I would trade *The Shell Book* in for his *Selected Insects*.

3

mantis on a muskmelon

His mantis has about it an intentness; whether to eat
or put it off till later, its urgent task is to decoy.
Watch her posed on a muskmelon, head topped with feelers,
a headdress tipped towards the future, as she looks
with her all-seeing convex eyes and raises claws to pray.
She would trick me as she will certainly trick him,
the small cone-headed grasshopper incapable
of strategy, blind to his fate. No one comes out

and says it; no commentary alludes. Those who sat
on riverbanks shuffling their sly, erotic, night-time topics,
those who floated poems under bridges and those who
read them, simply knew it. Most of his insects are women.

4

a suitor's lines

Men pen the verses that attend these plates.
In front of Utamaro's captivating creatures, and foliage
so alive each swaying stalk might stand in for a verb,
their lines take wing. Love is the all-embracing subject.
One wistful wooer entrusts his feelings to a paper
that he rolls up 'like a coiled snake'; and in the next line
lets himself be lured into describing pent-up passion
as 'deep as the length of that [by now uncoiled] snake'.

A slender-waisted suitor muses on a thin, red insect body ...
a dragonfly is burning away as he is, both
of them love-wasted, wordlessly bearing
the weight of a lover's pain.

5

likenesses and old lines

Each reflection is quickened by a likeness.
When *kyōka* stands on *haiku*, old lines take the meaning on.
A lover finds release from longing in a cleverly
charged pun. The lithe incumbent of the final plate,
a true frog surfacing from water,
draws from the poet the figure of a go-between
who shakes off her commission like drops
of water splashing on the face of a frog.

Hers is an insouciance that paints over nature's
real indifference. It summons Bashō, only to upend
his brief, indelible alignment of an old pond
with the sound of a jumping frog.

6

bagworm and scarab

The *minomushi* hatches in spring and starts to weave a case
from what's to hand. She grows a dwelling tailored to her needs,
one she can move around in, fastened with her silk.
By winter, branches will be strung with these self-woven houses.
Hers is a chandelier that drops in icicles from its host tree,
but it hangs from a spray weighted with flowers; their two-tone
pink, their turning leaves, insist upon late summer.   The scarab
stands on the tossing deck of a plantain lily's leaves.

His little horns reach up unevenly, in awkward yearning.
The placing is refined (genre, like genus, prescribes no two
should touch). I wouldn't say it's non-committal – rather,
for the beetle, the bagworm is as far off as a star.

7

rat snake and skink

They play upon leaf-pads, crawl along stems or duck
below a canopy of leaves. A pair, at times a triangle, will share,
as lovers would, a double page. So does desire come into it?
I think at times it must, though on these lavish surfaces
we will not see them touch. Desire, its route varied as gender ...
take that rat snake and a skink – the slide of mottled scales
through rioting dayflower, the lizard's edginess, the snake's encircling
glide, are clues to imminent connection. He holds it there,

at a thin line flicked from her blunt mouth towards
his stiffened tail, but hints at more. Whether a day
or night-time thing, in this or any shape desire
will hold a sense of what's in store.

8

they gather and merge

For trust and for community we must await his women.
They gather like foliage. To the side of a triptych one girl is held up
by another, a third girl at their feet, while they raid a tree
for fruit. Autumn tonings bind them, persimmon
and persimmon picker, as they go about their chores.
They are made of ovals and of oblongs. I watch them merge
into the sort of plump and patterned caterpillar
you would uncover clinging to a stem in Utamaro's *Insects*.

And the poet-suitor? In the evenings we hear him calling
like any garden creature from its bank, and think
back to the grasshopper they call 'horse-driving', the one
who stretches out towards his love the reins of his small heart.

The act of ending

two figures similar in size
take up the stage
his part will prevail

you can see it in the colours
of his narrowly striped robe   maroon
yellow   green   maroon

he stands over her
hunched like an owl   extending
a fine-boned hand

towards the breast   which has
fallen   a rounded rock
out of her kimono   when

as though to hold him
she reached for the tie at his waist
and her robe   opened

its yellow silk   spotted
with the first strokes of blossom
a downpour of petals

that cradles her skin   channel
of face   into neck   into chest
a lining spills

over her bared leg
and pools below it like
the rippling of shallow waters

a method of painting   applied
to undersilk
when the wind   stills   waves quieten

as they contemplate the act
that follows (it is the act
of ending)

both delicate faces show concern
          only   she
is haunted by his power to leave

for her there is no crossroads
this is what I know of relationships
human or not

III

FIFTEEN POEMS ON THINGS: TRANSLATIONS

1

the wind

Gently intermittent, it draws the red bud from its case;
Its thick mass spread, green cocklebur is stirred.
Drooping willows bend and then rise up;
Young duckweed comes together, to disperse.
In the corridor long sleeves are blown about;
Facing the door, with thoughts of throwing wide lapels.
The clear high notes of flute and song float out;
Longing thoughts of which you do not know.
Often I dust the single simurgh mirror.
Hair at my temples shows flecked with stars.

2

the bamboo

Before the window a single thicket of bamboo.
Standing alone, its fresh young green is striking.
Upper branches cross with lower leaves;
New shoots dot its aged limbs.
In the moonlight leaves sparse-etched then dense;
In the breeze it stretches up, then bends again.
Green finches freely dart about;
Fledglings can catch glimpses of each other.
One regret: its sheath, stripped by the wind,
From root and trunk is forever apart.

3

the rose bush

Low branches – how can they bear their leaves?
A light scent propitiously spreads itself.
Emerging buds, at first a tight-furled purple;
Late season's petals still rain red.
New buds face the bright sun;
Old blooms follow the movements of the wind.
Uneven limbs receive the sun by turns;
Who would remark this humble little bush?

4

the rushes

Rushes lying thick along the water;
Pools on their surface scatter into pearls.
In autumn, lotus flowers in their midst;
In spring the baby ducks weave in and out.
Early buds fill the carved stands;
Last blooms are mixed to plaster the Pepper Rooms.
Sad the song 'On the Embankment':
'In the end they will wear away gold.'

5

the dodder

A light silk that will form no pattern;
Fine threads that will never weave.
Dispersing into a thousand shimmering strands;
Forming a stretch of silk, again one hue.
You cannot know where it will set its roots,
Nor guess at where it will entwine its heart.
Prized for its rolling up and stretching out,
Why should it heed the tumbleweed and grow up straight?

6

falling plum blossom

Young leaves reach delicately down;
New buds shed a first sweet scent.
Meeting you at a Rear Park banquet;
Following sweet smiles, returned.
Engaging your own jade-white fingers;
Plucked, to present to Nan Wei.
Held to place in a cloudy hair-coil;
The jade hairpins compete with their gloss.
At day's end, falling, fading for ever;
Your favour cannot be regained.

7

visiting the eastern hall; composed on the paulownia there

Outside the north window is a lone paulownia;
High branches reach over a hundred feet.
Its leaves grow in a thick profusion;
When they fall [branches] spray and spread.
It has neither fruit nor flowers –
What to send to my parted love?
Fashioned into tablets of jade
It once served to command all of Shen.

8

the gardenia on the north wall

A lovely tree faces the courtyard steps;
Frost and dew are powerless to injure it.
On massed gold fruit vermilion hues break through;
Reflecting the sun, to seem denser still.
Fortunately it can rely on the sun's declining rays;
The last light reaches its western-most limbs.
It longs to be reflected in the limpid waters –
No curved pool before your courtyard steps.
Its lingering brilliance is not yet over –
Late season's fruit appears wonderful.
Retaining its virtue when gathered in the basket;
Your favour's extent truly cannot be known.

9

the *qin*: seven-stringed zither

By Dong Ting lake a trunk worn by wind and rain;
At Long Men hill boughs neither alive nor dead.
Cut and close-carved across its surface
Its strings sound a clear high plaint.
A spring breeze ripples through sweet clover;
An autumn moon fills Flowery Pool.
This time they play 'The Departing Crane'
And the listeners' tears flow streaming down.

10

the black leather armrest

A twisted trunk, from which limbs spring;
How could it not be carved and shaped?
Modelled on the dragon-patterned tripod,
Three-legged, it reveals a splendid form.
Do not speak of the purity of white skins;
White sand is subject to mutation still.
I offer a bent form of little use –
May it support you, weary, to the feast's end.

11
the mat

It grows up by the ebbing, flowing sea;
Last rays pick out its broken, serried lines.
Where pollia carpets the sandbars,
And lovage takes over secluded isles.
Encountering you, plucking and gathering;
On the jade couch where the golden goblet is offered.
One wish: to be swept by silken robes,
And not cause the pale dust to collect.

12
the bamboo brazier

Snow in the courtyard swirls like blossom;
Ice in the well turns to gleaming jade.
For its warmth the sable sleeve is placed upon it;
Embracing heat, it receives the fragrant quilt.
Though its form is dense, its function is to pass through;
Though its pattern slants, its nature will not warp.
It came from a village South of the River;
Slenderly swaying, tall and green.
Receiving for a time your jade-white fingers,
May it give way to the first beams of the spring sun.

13

the mirror stand

Lines clear-carved like vermilion railings;
Length looming like the Dark Watchtower,
The clear ice hangs from a phoenix pair;
The bright moon drops from flanking dragons.
It gives back a powdered face; she dusts it with rouge;
Places flowers in her hair, adjusts a cloud-like coiffure ...
A lovely face stares – to what end – at itself.
Always she fears the ending of his love.

14

the lamp

Emerald glints glance off the River of Stars;
Treasure stored on the crest of Mount Dang.
Stretching up its stem like an immortal's palm,
Its fire contained like the candledragon's.
A flying moth making three or four circles;
Light petals, four or five deep.
I face it, along with the evening's longings;
Vainly stitch by its light a dancing dress.

15

the candle

Under the gingko beams guests not yet scattered;
In Cassia Palace the light grows dim.
A faint glow from within the thin curtain;
Falling rays light a jewel-studded zither.
Wavering her hair mass's shadow;
Dazzling brilliant on filigree gold.
How, on an autumn-moon evening,
Could you leave me to my bedchamber's gloom?

IV

Compared to silence

I am holding *Hamlet* in my hands. A play of foils,
true and poisoned, scaffolds a death scene.
In swordplay someone must cede.   I, too,
am up against the notion of assignment; in a side
chapel of my mind, movements of the requiem
glow, rich in story, faceted as Hamlet.
To be is to be proof of paradox. The Sanctus
rises, its *in excelsis* all I'd ever want of glory.
Then comes the Pie Jesu   like
the clincher of some theory of existence

hatched by my reading. Music extends its sanction.
The text, an undertow, I knew before I started.
Who would not hear it: interwoven with
his choirs of angels the *requiem aeternam*?
It couldn't get more peace-on-earth than this.
Yet it will come, the judgement.   Midway
through, the great precautionary fanfare,
a thump of warning issued by the trombones
to a mind *Thou wouldst not think* intent on doing
two things *how ill all's here about my heart.*   Words

have taken over, a brimming handful spread
across a scene, rejecting and quiescent
the readiness is all   amounting to the compass
of a life   and so   *report me and*
my cause aright. Life now sinking into silence.
In those frontoparietal regions where
there is presently no talk of mind, the brain
needs quiet. The In Paradisum has arrived.
Caught up in a concert of activities, astray
among unanchored images,

I clutch at snippets: the brain is set to run
activities in sequence; the brain is occupied by
modules that joggle even-handedly within
the tin hat of the skull; the brain needs silence.
I am acquiring by the line the blocks
of a ramshackle theory. Do I think I am
the lyric's own Tom Stoppard, primed
to air ideas that prance, competitors
in an arena? Is it just that I am
holding *Hamlet* in my hands?

They have discovered the grail of attention.
They've seen it flickering in bordering regions of the brain.
What would they say to the suggestion of a nexus,
a frail and temporary alliance that links
the thoughts that launch themselves
from the page upwards and music as it filters
through the subtle networks of my brain?
I wait like any student for a simple answer.
Am I licensed to split attention,
to listen while I read?

While it lived

Sunset has drawn a single calligraphic line
through domes of backlit cloud and the true blue
of the sky. Brushed across the heavens,

it looks as if it held some kind of answer.
Before I can decipher it, a cloud has put out blunted
paws and smudged the feathered outline.

While it lived, it was intensity itself.
But it was short-lived as a wave and, like a wave,
turned out to have no other message.

The critic at sunset

They cling like snow to the line of the hill,
their proportion that of wave top
to its wave. Perched on a point,
the houses are an outpost. Just a strip
of habitation holding fast above
the massive plates on which they balance,
like one brave mind engaging
with the savage present.

The critic in him sweeps through shelves,
pouncing on those words that come unbidden;
these (after Dryden) he pronounces 'hits'.
Brimming with connections, he looks to praise,
where he can find it, craft. He is vital
before time and illness, and when he thinks
a line, or he himself can bear it, offers
a glimpse of the last great human theme.

On its promontory, the strip of houses
flames at sunset. It makes a cultivated stand
against raw statement. Will it ebb, will it increase?
Are his lines over? We, who are sure of nothing,
see this present lapped in burnished distance:
cliffs brittle as bone, the hard-to-read
stance of the land, the role played in all
of this by an ever-ambiguous sea.

Empty your head

1

You know the old charts that they eased from adventurers'
tales in the days when the sun still circled the earth –
where whole strips of coastline were guesswork
and a fanfare of graphics showcased snippets from story,
where, if Caliban waited invention, other old-fashioned
monsters roamed emptied interiors, or spouted
in misshapen seas? Pictured in bubbles stuffed
with allusion were snatches of history drawn from
the annals. The images made up a world.
That world was the map-maker's own.

Bit by bit it was peeled away. There was pain
in the process – for the thinkers, explorers,
the sceptics. Their pain was appalling but they leaned
on the overfilled charts as if they were pillars.
Stretched them like Samson, stopping just short
of ruin. Only then could it enter, incontestable
space. How it whitened the parchment.
Now a mind could stray west or drift south.
An eye might look up at the sky.
Discovery follows a vacuum.

We learnt then how an innocent map
could be dipped in the harsh dyes of empire.
It had happened before, whenever
a centre – despotic, right-minded, regardless –
got its hands on peripheral peoples.
Exploration, encounter, commerce, control.
A map never shows any sequence,
no hint of a fault line, no crack
between empires.
A map simply shows how it ended.

2

Add the word science and spot the new driver
abetting possession; we're talking vast swathes of the globe.
Once more there were graphics in virgin interiors.
Fantastic avians sang from the parchment.
An array of odd animals stalked the cleared surfaces.
When the bubbles began to enfold different data
we saw how perspectives had changed.
There were words like 'extinct', some prefaced
with tags – 'hunted to' was a favourite.
That was the dark side.

It had gone on across the new globe.
Take terra australis; gripped by an ingrained vision,
they said there was nothing there.
Had they heard of the land that was no land,
a featureless plane that waited in darkness?
Had they merely failed to catch up?
They had not; they knew nothing of any Dreaming,
when the Ancestor Beings, having broken the crust
of that surface, created the landscape
with everything in and around it, then retired

transformed to their sites. The surveyors
saw few signs of occupation. Unable to read
the rich crisscross of animal, human, and spirit tracks,
they missed traces left from the Dreamtime.
They earmarked the land for themselves.
Anthropologists started to study the peoples.
Collectors began with their art.
Helped by its flight to paper, they came,
when directed, to see the progress of Emu –
one of a handful of creatures whose steps led

out of the past to conclude in a dried-up creek.
Would it offer a way in, or back, this art
that looked more like a map? Each painting aligned
with a story from an ancient, peopled, land.
Would we come, when taught, to grasp
in the dots and their circulation, a country-
wide songline, a passage through the high stars?
Would we come to understand,
we who will never inhabit a songline
or follow a desert track?

coda

When we go about salvage, and mean it,
will they ask that we empty the map
again, that we go back and
empty the map?

They can see that it's too late for that.
They will ask in its place for room,
space for themselves and their stories
swept from the face of the land.

Let us sit alongside
as we empty a place in our heads
as once we had emptied
the maps.

We are not accountable for myth

1

These peaks are half robed, stage goddesses,
snow raked through their thighs.

Their sharp gothic faces are upthrust. Aggressive –
or more to be pitied, like Guo Xi's twisted trees?

The peaks point nowhere; neither looking up in worship
nor marking any kind of terminus for the eye.

Swathes of foothill moat a fixed community,
making of the peaks a city. On its eastern flank,

a furnace-glow is painting unscalable sides. Some earth-
effort is going on below. Above, the light is angry,

clouds flare, a giant wing of orange overcomes their pink.
Leave this turning bird, measureless as the mythic Peng.

2

A pool is a dual experience; it toys with the idea of reflection.
In this foreground, the water's lavender-tinged pink

returns a dream: the memory of some cloud-based action
as affecting as hers when she rode her horse, Grane,

into fire, the side of her face flame-lit,
you'd say transcendent, while the magnified head

of him who caused it all fades from the screen.
We are not accountable for myth. Any myth.

But the old anguished world –
should you kick off against it with your heels,

an oar, still held by its beauty?

New identity stories

1

these days you can do anything
linger out loud over your common or
garden genitalia   which was once

to say identity   your uncommon
gender   which complicates it
for us all

2

these days you can do anything
bring in Proust but who does   luxuriate
as if for the first time

over the luscious stretch
of a sentence
all you can do is let it rise

The undeflected

1

when we   shielded by sea
and our own good intentions   talk
trust   they laugh at platitude

the idea of community
as we pronounce it   here
they are against

though we shape ideas
in their image
nothing we say will

change
their minds
they are the undeflected

2

trammelled by life
they put their stamp   on words
and conspire to pierce evidence

expect them one day to unite
and make their bid   as all along
they would have liked

understand how   at that moment
they aspire   to become   more
than the undeflected

The unprepared

tugged back into the wreckage
this turning morning
sleepless as a plant

we speculate where the thought-arrows
had they been allowed through
might have landed

What a poem cannot be

he is looking out over lashing sea
as he scrabbles with bare hands
for words she will not hear

he unjoins seams in the salt air
his object   all
they are capable of saying

no one can coax from them meaning
enough   meaning   his mind
a wave on the point of breaking

he cuts despair
into a base of anguish
as you cut butter into flour

if you knew his life   his loss
you would see that
his is a rending from the root

upwards   he knows only
what a poem cannot be
it is not her landscape   will not

be mine   though I go to it
back and back to it
understanding less each time

Between the sky and land

in memoriam J

1

The boy is a perfect fifteen. He is poised against sky,
sea and land. This is how his mother saw him
when she captured him that last time –
modelling an ancient triad made
of heaven, the earth, and man.

The boy stands there like David.
Battle-ready in his head. About the same age,
and sifting through what in his world to confront.
A cloud-whitened sky, a blue block of sea,
grey-green strip of a sun-soaked land.

And the boy stands there like David,
a boy who is not yet a man.

2

The excitement of shock came first. Winded
by thoughts of his own, he rushed out of his house,
in step with some on-the-spot plan. He ran down –
as if drawn to the balm of the harbour. Impulse
takes over the brain like the red that takes over the trees.

He ran like a hero in search of solution.
That night he went over a bridge.
Strode, faltered, was pushed – the hard sides
of the cliffs are shrouded in cloud,
giving nothing away.

3

Those closest to him can find no verbs
to trust. Stricken, bereft, unable
to believe, they have no words
at all. They have nothing
to stopper sorrow.

4

It rises from the finest of pipes,
a perpetual lament in the ear.
It rises, renewing itself, in the karakia.
Banners of red and blue sunlight reach
as far as the flowers on the coffin.

His great-uncle, head of the clan,
is a gentle white bird in his surplice. Day
offers what comfort it can – light
brims in the spaces between us.
Near the end of the service

I think of my brother opening his arms to
his grandson, there, in the place where
he landed. The sides of the cliffs in the spot
where he fell, are still shrouded in cloud.
Unappeased, giving nothing away.

Canterbury contrapuntal

a wedding song for Jonty and Letitia

In Hagley Park the red and yellow tide of autumn
has long since ebbed and, in a sarabande along the Avon,
English trees shake from their bared arms
last clinging vestiges of leaf. The bordering bush
acts out a different, hidden, drama – its merged greens
merely darken; they will see the winter through.

In Bath and Wiltshire there's no room for anything but flowers.
Flowers fill summer fields and pivot on the tiered cake.
Each flower contributes its own meaning, Shakespeare tells us.
And, as in his shepherds' scene, the coming days will be all
flowers and feasting, dancing in the meadows of high summer.
Among the featured props are graceful tractors Shakespeare
never dreamed of, as he romped among polarities and played off
human difference. Here are Canterbury sheep as plump as
bushes. A whole history of connection lies in the echoed name.
Today joins opposite geographies, as though two sides of the earth
have lifted and come together, like sides of a picnic rug.
Dark yang has merged with pale yin as lovingly and cleanly
as on the ancient symbol.
                  And here comes Maisie –
how her brown eyes shine. Her hold on newborn Elsie is relaxed,
as if she'd found this sister, like a precious pebble, on some lawn
or beach. Today, flowers thread her autumn-coloured hair.
They blend with those her mother carries. Maisie holds her own.
It looks as if, like Shakespeare's Perdita, she'll offer you
a choice: love and friendship, lasting union, joy.

Walking during lockdown

1

(in Karori Cemetery)

The prodigal summer sun has left for good, replaced
by autumn stillness. We enter and move through as if we had
brought in from our curbed world the idea of compliance.
White wooden crosses at the end of graves, footnotes

to the fact of death, point to those who died a century ago
in the pandemic. Most upright, some askew, the crosses
stand today in ghostly correspondence. I stop reading
the names. I look up to the massed tops of trees,

bushy or frayed, each stencilled on its ground of sky.
If I let my eyes slide down the runnelled trunks,
it is to end at hollows spread with a fresh burnt orange
straw. Here, no one looks below the surface.

2

(in the Botanic Garden)

Autumn is a suite, alternating measures, sedate
with energetic. If we began it with a sarabande,
we would call this one a gigue – paths stream

with leaves, creeks pour in a multi-coloured current
over every small stone dam or barrier. It is clear
where this is heading. The gigue comes at the end.

We want it to stop there, before the stasis
and the silence, the frozen hush of winter; to stop
at the acacia still patched with green,

with a small girl swinging herself on a branch, swinging,
swinging, like a Spanish child let out of lockdown;
with the world taking a break, as it had to.

March–May 2020

Accommodations

for Swan

1

She has walked through the Gardens to the camellias,
to where tiers of steps part the glossy bushes
and she is encircled by leaves. It is the same
and always different. Above her, a white magnolia;
each year it throws up, with its tide of flowers,
some distinctive conceit. She is thinking
of me – we were children encircled
by stories. It is too cold to meet.

A voice has cancelled the blaze. The magnolia
lifts emptied branches to colourless sky.
It has held back its crop – just a few tight buds
then it wavered. A connection has thinned
and failed. She doesn't know why. The hill
to her right links suburbs like sections of spine.
The tree, as the crow flies, is equidistant
between her house and mine.

2

I stand in the place where she stood
and conjured likeness. On a grid of limbs
which the sun has edged with navy, a flock
of white unfolding bodies, smooth ovoids
that have settled there like birds. Wings
down, chests up, or is it throats extended –
what is it they extol? Here's passion
enough to reinvent the whole tradition.

Come on, John Donne, come Hopkins –
what, this year, do they bring?
A splash of camellia, crimson in a corner
of a print; a refined asymmetry that must be
Japanese. An enduring play of pattern
and, threading the air, the lovely
accommodations of friendship,
the stabbing start of spring.

The excitable

unseamed by ignore
you wilt   the sun airborne
against your hand

the excitable are   blinded
by light   they need water
not   transcendence

Irish girls

for Rhian Gallagher

You have been talking a sun-bleached slope, the brilliant scatter
of small flowers. You must have been walking, running,
rolling through long grass, quaking grass,
the yellowing blades of summer grass. *Anyone's childhood.*

As you go on, I feel you become what you say
of a trickle swelling in its mind to a mighty gush, of a floor
parqueted with ferns – one with whatever looks up
to a spread of sky canopied, or not, by the bush.

*

'Bush' is the kind of diminutive that doesn't let on.
You need not throttle delight on its outskirts;
look at that plump fool, the kererū – again and again
it appears close up, as though in garden play.

The bush is deception. There is no deep centre;
you quail before its reach. The bush is three parts
isolation and one part danger. As much as any
old world forest it collapses into allegory.

The mass of the subject pushes against you.
It pulses through a mush of gravel; it branches into
streams that ripple over what you came to learn.
Now it comes with the tip tap tap

of a beak on bark, a hunch
that is finding its way into the open.
Like a ghost that braves the sunlight or the stage,
your Irish voice breaks through.

*

You are not so much feet in the peat as Heaney,
who reached down and brought up fine-faced corpses
burnished by ordeal until they shone; then blent them
with lived atrocities, relayed with a compassion

that scorched. But anyone can hear it, that self-same pity,
in your scenes from the asylum. *The girl's insane*, they say,
their verdict executed with the slower kind of savagery.
When history moves to archive, the drivers disappear.

You pull up the blind on absence, lovesickness and desertion,
the wrenching splits that widen over the years.
You return us to the peat, the bush, the bifurcation,
girl upon Irish girl abandoned to a loosely worn despair.

*

A scrawny southern rātā sways outside a hut.
In a dip in the hills, a dish of light wells below bunched
cloud. Just before darkness, the tree is transformed.
As you turn your head, its far-off promise

is swabbed away like so much wash – not before
you know it is your kind of grail and you'd follow it
anywhere, although now it is night and the bush
is three parts danger and one part isolation.

*

You burst from the top of the track like cresting rock.
Secure as crannied moss, held there, sky-
high, by the poet's knack of integration. Without it,
you might walk out over nothing, into the blue.

ACKNOWLEDGEMENTS

I acknowledge the example of Seamus Heaney, who began his volume of poetry *Seeing Things* (London: Faber & Faber, 1991) with a partial translation of *The Aeneid* Book VI.

I would like to thank Joan Mirviss, who generously presented me with a copy of the book on which the sequence in Section II of the collection is based: *Utamaro: Songs of the Garden*, with an introduction, notes and translation by Yaksuko Betchaku and Joan B. Mirviss (New York: The Metropolitan Museum of Art and The Viking Press, 1984).

That this present collection draws together poems and translations, I owe to two generous and percipient friends, each of whom recognised the seamlessness that can exist between a translated poem and one that emerges from a writer's head.

I have always been drawn to work that is compressed and allusive, and to poems that lean on images. This way of constructing a piece frees it to be as spare as a tree in winter. But it was Duncan Campbell, one of New Zealand's leading sinologists, who connected the small-scale topics and compressed formats of the Chinese verse I had once studied to descriptive precision in my own poems. I went on to make other connections. Among them I saw that I would often structure a poem with a 'scene statement' placed in the 'head' and/or 'belly' of the poem, and a personal response located in the 'tail' – in the way of the Chinese lyric. And so, I began to realise what my eye might reach for as a topic, and what was attractive to me as a poet. From such conversations a writer's poetics begins to emerge.

I had written most of the poems that comprise this collection when Robert Easting, Emeritus Professor of English, suggested that I add a group of my translations. These were 'poems on things'. He didn't need to say that the collection already contained a number of poems written in response to objects. Some, like the gravel chips and bits of shell pounced on by a baby, are actual objects. In more elevated vein, I consider a head of the Buddha, a painting by Pissarro, a recent collection of poems by Rhian Gallagher, all addressed as objects of interest. It seemed I had written my own poems on things.

With them came ways of looking carried over, or developed, from my reading of the Chinese lyric. The topics that form the material world of the court poet – the bamboo and plum blossom, the musical instruments, mirror stands and candles – operate in a certain way. An object-topic will evoke and then retreat before an idea, leaving it the floor. Many of my poems reach for connections. They are stranded with references, and bring large questions with them, usually in their final lines.

I was persuaded by Robert's idea that the translations might not only open a window into late fifth-century Chinese writing but also shed light on my own. As a result, this collection took on its present form. Working on it has brought me a wonderfully satisfying sense of life's having come full circle.

A word on 'poems on things'

My translations of fifteen short 'poems on things' by Chinese poet Xie Tiao (464–499) make up Section III of the book. Although I hope that the poems can speak for themselves, the following background, including a brief evocation of the kind of situation in which they were written, might help to sharpen their reading.

'Poems on things' are a subgenre of the main lyric form. They were usually impromptu, composed in a group situation on objects in front of the eyes. Strict time limits were brought to bear, as an example taken from *History of the Southern Dynasties* shows:

> The Prince of Jingling [Xiao] Ziliang [460–494] used to hold evening gatherings of literati. A candle would be notched to determine the length of a poem; for a poem of four rhymes [i.e., an eight-line poem], the cut was made an inch down the candle, and this was used as a marker.

Such demands threw the poet back on precedent. Fortunately, an education aimed at an acquaintance with the entire tradition made sure that the pertinent poetic precedents lay at his fingertips.

In these poems, the 'thing' in question – falling plum blossom, a brazier placed in a wide sleeve, a seven-stringed instrument or the name of a song – will summon and then give way to an idea: love, loyalty, abandonment.

Description takes centre stage until the poet's persona, which is often that of a woman, emerges, typically in the last couplet.

The poems are characterised by a wit that not only plays with meaning but extends to their structure. Most are composed as an indirect answer to the question 'what am I?', which makes of them a kind of riddle.

An audience might admire the wit on offer, but it also wants to be moved. The poet responds with allusion. In 'The Qin: seven-stringed zither' (no. 9), Xie Tiao introduces the name of a song, 'The Departing Crane'. Placed at a key point, the last couplet, the song and the story it holds sum up the poem's plaintive atmosphere and generate an added note of romantic sadness.

An emotional dimension enters with a female presence, which is suggested by a semi-erotic nuance, a literary reference, or even by association with a decorative object – a mirror stand or lamp. In 'The Candle' (no. 15), the reflection of a woman's hair morphs, in the last couplet, into direct complaint. Somewhere between lies the woman herself. She is both stereotype and newly imagined vehicle of an age-old resentment:

> Wavering her hair mass's shadow;
> Dazzling brilliant on filigree gold.
> How, on an autumn-moon evening,
> Could you leave me to my bedchamber's gloom?

Readers who would like to know more about these poems can see my book *An Unexpected Legacy: Xie Tiao's 'Poems on Things'* (Wellington: Asian Studies Institute and the New Zealand Centre for Literary Translation, Victoria University of Wellington, 2008). This contains the Chinese texts, these translations, comprehensive footnotes and a prefatory essay.

NOTES

Epigraphs: The quotation by Theodor W. Adorno is from *Negative Dialectics* (London: Continuum Press, 1973). The one by W.G. Sebald is from his foreword to *A Place in the Country* (London: Hamilton, 2013); 'his pictures' refers to work by the German artist Jan Peter Tripp.

He has put away pointers responds to Camille Pissarro's *Le Champ de choux, Pontoise*, 1873. www.museothyssen.org/en/collection/artists/pissarro-camille/cabbage-field-pontoise

The title of **Singing robes** glances off William Empson's phrase about Wordsworth putting on his 'singing robes'.

In **A butterfly floats in the paint**, the painting under discussion is Simon Kaan's *Circle*, in oil on wood. It is owned by my daughter Susannah and her husband, Paul Robinson. Gus was their cat. 'Zhuangzi' refers to the fourth-century BCE Chinese philosopher Zhuang Zhou, whose butterfly dream is well known:

> Once Chuang Chou dreamt he was a butterfly, a butterfly flitting and fluttering around, happy with himself and doing as he pleased. He didn't know he was Chuang Chou. Suddenly he woke up and there he was, solid and unmistakable Chuang Chou. But he didn't know if he was Chuang Chou who had dreamt he was a butterfly, or a butterfly dreaming he was Chuang Chou. Between Chuang Chou and a butterfly there must be *some* distinction! This is called the Transformation of Things. (*The Complete Works of Chuang Tzu*, translated Burton Watson (Columbia: Columbia University Press, 1968).)

The flying creatures was written in response to an episode of the 2019 TV miniseries 'Judi Dench's Wild Borneo Adventure'. The three protagonists were Dame Judi, ecologist Eleanor Slade, and Bob, a dung beetle. I dedicate the poem to them all. Dame Judi has further acknowledged the occasion with a paean to Bob Beetle:

The praises I feel must be sung
To Bob Beetle who carries the dung
It was love at first sight
On that warm muggy night
In Borneo a country far flung!

The poems in **Utamaro's Objects** respond to artworks by the Japanese artist and designer Kitagawa Utamaro (1753–1806). His studies of the natural world preceded the paintings of elegant women of 'the floating world', *ukiyo-e*, for which he became better known.

In the New York Public Library: *Gifts from the Ebb Tide* (also known as *The Shell Book*) (*c.* 1789) combines Utamaro's polychrome woodblock prints with poems. The 'one page' referred to in the poem is the double-page illustration 'Shell gathering'. www.metmuseum.org/art/collection/search/57648

Songs of the garden: *The Book of Insects* (or *Picture Book of Selected Insects*) (1788) combines Utamaro's woodblock prints with some thirty *kyōka* compiled by Yadoya no Meshimori. *Kyōka* (狂歌 'wild' or 'playful poems') is a humorous subgenre of the *tanka*. This compressed form, which reached the height of its popularity in the last decades of the eighteenth century, offered multiple opportunities for ambiguous play. www.metmuseum.org/art/collection/search/78742

In **true forms**, the line 'where there are flowers there should be / butterflies, as a fine lady is accompanied by her maids' is taken from the Chinese painting manual *The Mustard Seed Garden*.

bagworm and scarab: *minomushi* is the Japanese name for the bagworm; the 'host tree', in this print, is the Japanese bushclover.

they gather and merge: *Picking Persimmons, c.* 1802–4. From a triptych of woodblock prints, ink and colour on paper, by Utamaro. www.metmuseum.org/art/collection/search/37280

'The katydid, or long-horned grasshopper is nicknamed "horse driving" in Japan ... because of its shape' ('Commentary on the Poems', *Utamaro: Songs of the Garden*).

The act of ending: *Parting of Lovers: Courtesan and Her Lover, c.* 1800, a polychrome woodblock print by Utamaro. www.metmuseum.org/art/collection/search/37314

The lines in italics also come from *The Mustard Seed Garden*.

the rushes: 'Pepper Rooms' are the empress's apartments. This line refers to the practice of mixing the flowers of the pepper plant with mud to make a fragrant plaster to spread on the walls of the empress's quarters.

The song 'On the Embankment' was attributed to the Empress Zhen (183–221), second wife of Cao Pi (187–226), who became Emperor Wen of Wei. Cao Pi encountered her after the defeat in battle of her first husband and was much taken with her beauty. He subsequently married her although her former husband was still alive. After the birth of the Empress Zhen's two children, Cao Pi's affections wandered. She enraged him with her complaints and was eventually ordered to commit suicide. Variant versions of 'On the Embankment' all contain the lines around which 'The Rushes' is built:

> The rushes grow in my pond;
> How lushly thick their leaves ...
> Ill-report will wear away gold,
> Cause you to live a life parted from me ...

In **visiting the eastern hall; composed on the paulownia there**, Shen is the star realm identified with the three great stars which, in the Western tradition, comprise the Belt of Orion. The region that corresponds to Shen was the ancient state of Jin, principally located in modern Shanxi Province.

The critic at sunset was written during Clive James' final months. James once wrote, 'Dryden had a name for the happy phrase that came unbidden: he called it a hit. "These hits of words a true poet often finds ... without seeking; but he knows their value when he finds them, and is infinitely pleased."' (Clive James, 'A Stretch of Verse', *Poetry Notebook: 2006–2014* (London: Picador, 2014).)

We are not accountable for myth: The strange shapes of the trees of Northern Song landscape painter Guo Xi (*c.* 1020–1090) appear to have been twisted by wind or the struggle to maintain a foothold on precipitous cliffs.

Peng is the gigantic fish-turned-bird of Chinese mythology. 'The back of the P'eng measures I don't know how many thousand *li* across and, when he rises up and flies off, his wings are like clouds all over the sky.' (*The Complete Works of Chuang Tzu*, translated Burton Watson.)

Grane is Brünnhilde's horse in Wagner's Ring cycle; the poem refers to the final opera, *Götterdämmerung.*

Canterbury contrapuntal: 'shepherds' scene' refers to the sheep-shearing scene from Shakespeare's *The Winter's Tale.*

Irish girls was written in response to Rhian Gallagher's collection *Far-Flung* (Auckland: Auckland University Press, 2020), which calls in its first half on memories of a New Zealand childhood; and, in its second, enacts a play of voices, those of the young, mostly female, Irish migrants who were sent to the Seacliff Lunatic Asylum in the last decades of the nineteenth century.

Published by Otago University Press
533 Castle Street
Dunedin, New Zealand
university.press@otago.ac.nz
www.oup.nz

First published 2023
Copyright © Diana Bridge
The moral rights of the author have been asserted

ISBN 978-1-99-004854-8

Editor: Anna Hodge
Design: Fiona Moffat

Front cover: Miranda Joseph, *Teal*, 2016, Oil on canvas, 1600mm x 1600mm.
Collection of the Otago Polytechnic.

Printed in New Zealand by Ligare.